Randy Moss

Additional Titles in the Sports Reports *Series*

Roberto Alomar
Star Second Baseman
(0-7660-1079-1)

Charles Barkley
Star Forward
(0-89490-655-0)

Mark Brunell
Star Quarterback
(0-7660-1830-X)

Kobe Bryant
Star Guard
(0-7660-1828-8)

Terrell Davis
Star Running Back
(0-7660-1331-6)

Tim Duncan
Star Forward
(0-7660-1334-0)

Dale Earnhardt
Star Race Car Driver
(0-7660-1335-9)

Brett Favre
Star Quarterback
(0-7660-1332-4)

Kevin Garnett
Star Forward
(0-7660-1829-6)

Jeff Gordon
Star Race Car Driver
(0-7660-1083-X)

Wayne Gretzky
Star Center
(0-89490-930-4)

Ken Griffey, Jr.
Star Outfielder
(0-89490-802-2)

Scott Hamilton
Star Figure Skater
(0-7660-1236-0)

Anfernee Hardaway
Star Guard
(0-7660-1234-4)

Tim Hardaway
Star Guard
(0-7660-1500-9)

Grant Hill
Star Forward
(0-7660-1078-3)

Allen Iverson
Star Guard
(0-7660-1501-7)

Michael Jordan
Star Guard
(0-89490-482-5)

Shawn Kemp
Star Forward
(0-89490-929-0)

Jason Kidd
Star Guard
(0-7660-1333-2)

Michelle Kwan
Star Figure Skater
(0-7660-1504-1

Tara Lipinski
Star Figure Skater
(0-7660-1505-X)

Dan Marino
Star Quarterback
(0-89490-933-9)

Mark Messier
Star Center
(0-89490-801-4)

Reggie Miller
Star Guard
(0-7660-1082-1)

Chris Mullin
Star Forward
(0-89490-486-8)

Hakeem Olajuwon
Star Center
(0-89490-803-0)

Shaquille O'Neal
Star Center
(0-89490-656-9)

Gary Payton
Star Guard
(0-7660-1330-8)

Scottie Pippen
Star Forward
(0-7660-1080-5)

Jerry Rice
Star Wide Receiver
(0-89490-928-2)

Cal Ripken, Jr.
Star Shortstop
(0-89490-485-X)

David Robinson
Star Center
(0-89490-483-3)

Barry Sanders
Star Running Back
(0-89490-484-1)

Deion Sanders
Star Athlete
(0-89490-652-6)

Junior Seau
Star Linebacker
(0-89490-800-6)

Emmitt Smith
Star Running Back
(0-89490-653-4)

Sheryl Swoopes
Star Forward
(0-7660-1827-X)

Frank Thomas
Star First Baseman
(0-89490-659-3)

Chris Webber
Star Forward
(0-89490-799-9)

Tiger Woods
Star Golfer
(0-7660-1081-3)

Steve Young
Star Quarterback
(0-89490-654-2)

Randy Moss

Star Wide Receiver

Ross Bernstein

Enslow Publishers, Inc.

40 Industrial Road   PO Box 38
Box 398   Aldershot
Berkeley Heights, NJ 07922   Hants GU12 6BP
USA   UK

http://www.enslow.com

Library of Congress Cataloging-in-Publication Data

Bernstein, Ross.
Randy Moss: star wide receiver / Ross Bernstein.
        p. cm. – (Sports reports)
Includes bibliographical references (p.) and index.
ISBN 0-7660-1503-3
1. Moss, Randy—Juvenile literature. 2. Football players—United States—
Biography—Juvenile literature. [1. Moss, Randy. 2. Football players.
3. Afro-Americans—Biography.] I. Title. II. Series.
GV939.M67 B47   2001

796.332'092—dc21

    00-011176

Printed in the United States of America

10 9 8 7 6 5 4 3 2

To Our Readers:
We have done our best to make sure all Internet addresses in this book were active
and appropriate when we went to press. However, the author and the publisher have
no control over and assume no liability for the material available on those Internet
sites or on other Web sites they may link to. Any comments or suggestions can be sent
by e-mail to comments@enslow.com or to the address on the back cover.

Photo Credits: Courtesy of the *Charleston Daily Mail*, pp. 20, 25; Courtesy of
the *Charleston Daily Mail*. News photo by Tom Hindman, p. 18;
Courtesy of Marshall University's Sports Information Department, pp. 37,
43; Courtesy of Marshall University's Sports Information Department.
Photo by Brett Hall, Marshall University, 1996, p. 34; Courtesy of Marshall
University's Sports Information Department. Photo by Marilyn Testerman-
Haye, Marshall University, 1996, p. 39; Courtesy of Marshall University's
Sports Information Department. Photo by Rick Haye, Marshall University,
1996, p. 41; © Vincent Muzik, pp. 11, 52, 54, 56, 63, 67, 70, 72, 78, 89, 91.

Cover Photo: Illustration courtesy of Tim Cortes.

Contents

1 Busting Loose in Dallas. 7

2 Growing Up in West Virginia. 13

3 College Years. 29

4 Landing in Minnesota. 45

5 The NFL Rookie of the Year 59

6 A Sophomore Season to
Remember 75

7 The Future Is Bright. 87

Chapter Notes. 97

Career Statistics. 101

Where to Write and
Internet Addresses. 102

Index. 103

Chapter 1

Busting Loose in Dallas

Touchdown! That was a word that Dallas football fans were hearing way too much of on November 26, 1998. It was Thanksgiving Day in Dallas, and Minnesota Vikings rookie Randy Moss was giving the state of Texas absolutely nothing to be thankful for on this holiday.

The Vikings were coming off a big win over the Green Bay Packers the week before. They were eager to keep their league-best 10–1 record intact. After all, the Vikings were the hottest team in pro football. Randy Moss, their star wide receiver, had shown his talents to the Packers with 8 catches for 153 yards and one touchdown. He was quickly emerging as one of the game's biggest up-and-coming superstars.

Dallas, however, was also one of the favorites to win the championship. With a respectable 8–3 record, the Cowboys were riding a four-game winning streak. They were not about to get roughed up in their own backyard. Adding to the drama was the fact that Dallas had passed over Randy Moss just a few months earlier on draft day. Moss, who as a kid had dreamt of someday playing for the Cowboys, had not forgotten, either.

The game had all the excitement of the Super Bowl. It was Thanksgiving Day, and millions of fans from coast to coast were ready to sit down in front of the television after their big meal. The fans were hoping to see Dallas All-Pro cornerback Deion Sanders go one-on-one with Moss. At game time, however, Sanders was unable to play due to a sore foot. Nonetheless, the scene was wild at Texas Stadium, with the sold-out crowd ready to watch their Cowboys show the country why they were called "America's Team."

It did not take long for the Vikings' powerful offense to strike, and leading the charge was Randy Moss. At six feet four inches tall, he towered over Dallas's smaller defensive backs. He got things going early in the first quarter when he beat double coverage for a 51-yard touchdown on a pass from quarterback Randall Cunningham. The play started

FACT

Randy Moss is so popular that he has been chosen to be a Nike "Brand Jordan Athlete." Michael Jordan himself handpicked Moss as the only NFL player to carry on Jordan's brand of apparel with the same passion for play, style, and attitude. Moss's new sneaker line, called "Super-Freak," was released in summer 2000.

when Vikings running back Robert Smith took a handoff and faked a run. Instead, he pitched the ball back to Randall Cunningham. He heaved it up for the streaking Moss who had beaten both of his would-be defenders. The score was 7–0 before the game was even two minutes old.

After a 43-yard pass from Dallas quarterback Troy Aikman to Michael Irvin that set up a field goal, Cunningham came right back on Minnesota's second possession. This time, he hit Cris Carter over the middle for a 54-yard touchdown to make it 14–3. Still in the first quarter, Moss scored yet again, this time on a 56-yard touchdown bomb from Cunningham down the far sideline. Dallas again rallied on a pair of field goals and a 67-yard scoring pass from Aikman to Pat Jeffers. The Vikings then got a 45-yard field goal from kicker Gary Anderson just before halftime to give them a 24–16 lead.

Said Coach Dennis Green of Moss's second touchdown, "That's when I said, it's one thing to recognize a guy runs a 4.2 [40-yard-dash time], it's another to actually see him do it. To see a 4.2 is pretty amazing."[1]

Despite starting the second half with a comfortable lead, Minnesota was nervous. Its star running back, Robert Smith, had sprained his knee and would miss the rest of the game. Now, on the other side of the ball, Dallas's Pro Bowl running back, Emmitt Smith, got going in the second half. He scored a quick touchdown from two yards out to keep Dallas in the game. But backup Vikings running back LeRoy Hoard did not miss a beat. He scored on a 12-yard run immediately after a crucial pass-interference call on cornerback Kenny Wheaton for a 50-yard penalty.

Just minutes later, after another Dallas field goal, Randy Moss hauled in a short pass, shook off a tackle, and ran 56 yards for his third touchdown of the day. It was his ninth score of 40 yards or more that season.

"Every time I throw deep, I think he's going to catch it," said quarterback Randall Cunningham of Moss. "I throw it up there even when he's covered because he will go up and get it."[2]

Emmitt Smith then scored his second touchdown of the day on a short run up the middle. Hoard answered with a 50-yard run against the tiring Dallas defense. But Emmitt Smith kept his team alive, scoring his third touchdown of the day on a 4-yarder with 1:06 left in the game. It would be too little too late, though. Despite Smith's 3 touchdowns and Aikman's career-high 455 passing yards, Dallas could not find a way to stop Randy Moss. The Vikings went on to beat the Cowboys, 46–36. Randy

Once Randy Moss turns the corner on his defender, he is off to the races.

Moss, the hero of the game, was surrounded by his teammates.

Moss had 3 catches for 163 yards and 3 touch-downs, giving him a record 11 touchdowns and over 1,000 yards receiving for the year. After the game, Moss, who received NFC Offensive Player of the Week and Player of the Month honors, tried to keep it all in perspective.

"It was a great game and I'm just glad that we came out on top."[3]

With the win, Moss and the Vikings were ready to take home their first Central Division title in five years. Emotions were running high after the big game, as football fans everywhere could sense that something special was happening in Minnesota. Suddenly, many people were picking the Vikings to win the Super Bowl, thanks, in part, to the efforts of rookie Randy Moss.

Chapter 2

Growing Up in West Virginia

Born on February 13, 1977, Randy Moss grew up in Rand, West Virginia, a small mining community in the Kanawha Valley near the state capital of Charleston. Rand is located among the rolling hills and picturesque valleys of southwestern West Virginia. The town is home to several large chemical factories. The largest in the area, the DuPont plant, is in the neighboring town of Belle.

Moss was raised by his mother, Maxine, who worked very hard as a nurse's aide at the local hospital. She was a stern disciplinarian who made sure that her son grew up learning right from wrong. Maxine worked long hours and could not always be there, but she did not allow cursing in her home and she made sure that Randy attended church regularly. She felt it was very important to instill into her son the values that would make him a responsible young adult.

Randy did not live with his father, but he did have a male role model in the house to look up to—his half brother Eric. Three years older, Eric was a steadying influence in Randy's life. He was a very good student, a gifted athlete, and enjoyed playing sports with his little brother. Randy learned a lot from his half brother, and used to tag along to watch Eric's midget football and basketball games in the park. It was there that Randy grew to love competing.

As a young boy, Randy's idol was Chicago Bears Hall of Fame running back Walter Payton. "I idolized Walter Payton when I played Midget League," Moss said. "I respect him so much for the fact that he won a Super Bowl and he got out and made it happen."[1]

Randy entered the world of sports as a way to have fun and keep himself busy. A tall, fast youngster, Randy thrived in athletics at an early age. He loved to spend his free time playing all kinds of sports. As he grew older, it was not long before people could see that he had a lot of raw athletic ability. He excelled in youth leagues and even found the high school coaches coming to check him out when he was in grade school. He even excelled in pickup games with kids much older than he was. Whether it was on the football field, basketball court, baseball diamond, or asphalt track, Randy Moss seemed able to do it all.

In 1991, because Rand did not have a high school of its own, Moss attended DuPont High School in the neighboring town of Belle. In Rand, black students and white students went to school together. Belle, however, was mostly white. Randy was already well known for his athletic ability before he even got to high school. Some kids there were jealous of him. He was a new kid coming into a new school. Many of the white kids called him names and tried to get him to fight. It was nearly impossible for this six-foot four-inch African-American kid to just "blend in" and not stand out.

In the beginning, it was difficult for Moss to fit in, but he remembered the life lessons that he had learned from his mother and at church. He ignored the mean kids, and focused instead on being the best student-athlete that he could be.

In his first year at DuPont, Moss played football, basketball, and baseball, and even ran track as a sprinter. He excelled in all of these sports, earning

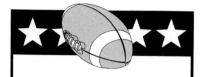

FACT

Believe it or not, Randy Moss was not the first professional sports "all-star" to come out of West Virginia. DuPont High School merged with East Bank High School in the late 1990s to form a new school called Riverside. Basketball Hall of Famer Jerry West went to East Bank. "Mr. Clutch," who led East Bank to the 1956 state championship, later led the University of West Virginia to the NCAA Finals in 1959, and the Los Angeles Lakers to the 1972 NBA title.

varsity letters in each. It was football, though, that would prove to be his best sport.

On the football field that fall, the wide receiver quickly learned how to use his superior size, speed, and moves to get open and score touchdowns. On the line of scrimmage, Moss would either blow past the smaller, slower cornerbacks defending him, or simply knock them over on his way downfield. Teams double-teamed him—put two defenders on him—trying to slow him down, but nothing worked. If he was double covered, that meant that one of his teammates was open somewhere down-field, waiting for an easy reception. If a ball was underthrown to him, he could leap and come back to it without even losing his stride. If a pass was thrown ahead of him, he would dive for it. Add to the mix his big, soft hands and incredible coordina-tion, and Randy Moss had the potential to be a legendary athlete.

Just how did Randy Moss do that first season at DuPont? He led the Panthers to the 1992 West Virginia State Championship that year over rival Brooke County. It was an amazing ride for the All-Conference and All-State selection, who made quite an impression on his teammates and coaches.

"We knew that Randy was something special

even before he got into high school," said DuPont head coach Dick Whitman.

> We had already coached his older brother Eric, who was an all-state fullback for us, and knew that his kid brother was going to be a star. We had been following Randy for quite some time as a youngster, watching him develop. We knew that he was very fast and had great hand-eye coordination. Plus, at six foot four in height, we knew that he was going to be an unbelievable force to be reckoned with out on the field.[2]

Moss also starred as a free safety on defense, where he quickly earned a reputation as a fierce defender and hard hitter. In addition to running back several interceptions for touchdowns that year, he became a secret weapon on the special teams—returning a couple of punts and kick-offs back for touchdowns.

"He never ceased to amaze us," said Coach Whitman. "As coaches, we were just trying to figure out how to get him the ball as much as humanly possible so that he could work his magic."[3]

When the football season was over, Moss went directly to the basketball court. There, the super sophomore lit up the hardwood like no one before him.

"We knew he was a phenom coming out of junior high school and couldn't wait to get him in a

Randy Moss led the DuPont Panthers to back-to-back West Virginia State Football titles in both 1992 and 1993.

varsity uniform," said DuPont's head basketball coach, Jim Fout. "Randy's leaping ability was amazing, and we saw early on that opposing teams just couldn't defend him with just one player."[4]

That year, Randy found himself getting amazing no-look passes from a small, but lightning quick, junior point guard. That guard was Jason Williams, who today plays for the NBA's Memphis Grizzlies. Williams and Moss instantly had a connection on and off the court. From alley-oops to monster jams and long-distance three-pointers, the duo became quite an attraction. The Panthers were knocked out of the playoffs that season. Nonetheless, Randy Moss had proved himself to be a real force among the best players in West Virginia.

"Having Randy as an athlete was a real joy," added Coach Fout.

> He was a tremendous talent and just a super kid. Not only was he an outstanding athlete, he was also a great person. He never missed a practice, always gave 100 percent on and off the court, and was a real competitor. Randy hated to lose and I think that is what really drove him to be a winner.[5]

After basketball season that year, Moss led the baseball team into the playoffs. In the process, he

Moss's friend and teammate Jason Williams (right) went on to stardom in the world of professional basketball playing for the NBA's Memphis Grizzlies.

proved to be a star center fielder and a clutch hitter. He was also a part-time pitcher, striking out his opponents. During the spring baseball season, Moss also ran track as a sprinter, and won the 100-meter-dash state title—proving without a doubt that he was indeed the fastest man in West Virginia.

That summer, Moss decided to focus primarily on football and basketball for the remainder of high school. One of the reasons for this was that his brother, Eric, himself an all-stater in both football and basketball, had recently earned a football scholarship to attend Ohio State University. He would play as an offensive lineman, tight end, and fullback. Inspired by his big brother, Randy Moss became determined to make it to the next level.

That next fall, Randy Moss came into football camp more determined than ever. He again led the way as the Panthers won another championship. This time, they beat Capital High School for the 1993 state title. For his efforts, Randy Moss once again earned All-Conference and All-State honors. He was now a superstar, and college scouts from across the country were eager to have him play for their schools.

As soon as the football season was over, Moss once again traded in his football cleats for his basketball sneakers. That season would prove to be a special one for the No. 2 ranked Panthers. Moss and Williams continued to entertain the fans. Fans would wait in line to make sure that they could get tickets to the games. More than 14,000 fans came to watch the team play its state quarterfinal game. The Panthers advanced to the Finals before losing to the top-ranked team from Martinsburg in the state championship game.

Randy Moss scored 587 points in 1994, the sixth-best single basketball season in school history. For his efforts he earned All-Conference and All-State honors. He was also named West Virginia's "Mr. Basketball"—an award honoring the state's best player. College scouts from coast to coast were now hoping to get Moss to come to their school.

Moss trained very diligently for the remainder of that school year. He lifted weights during the summer to get faster and stronger for the upcoming football season. By the beginning of his senior year, he was, without question, the most celebrated athlete in the state. His 44-inch vertical leap had earned him the nickname "Super-Freak" because of his almost inhuman athletic ability.

The two-time defending champs from DuPont were eager to win a third time. But they were beaten by South Charleston High School in the state semifinals. It was a sad ending for Randy Moss, but in addition to earning All-Conference and All-State honors that season Moss was also named the 1994 West Virginia Player of the Year. In his three seasons wearing the black and gold at DuPont, Moss averaged nearly 8 catches per game and scored more than 40 touchdowns. (That averaged out to be better than one touchdown per game.)

As soon as the football season ended, Moss once again got out on the basketball court. This year he was without his buddy Jason Williams, who had graduated and gone on to play at the University of Florida. Opposing players knew that if they beat Randy Moss one-on-one, they were simply beating the best.

Moss did not disappoint in his senior year. He led the Panthers to an impressive 19–5 record on the way to winning the state high school championship. More impressive was the fact that despite nearly every opponent double-teaming him that season, Moss averaged better than 30 points and 12 rebounds per game. He was also the team's leading three-point shooter. In the end he was once again named West Virginia's "Mr. Basketball." Randy Moss ultimately finished high school as

DuPont's all-time leading scorer with 1,713 career points.

Moss had decided to play only football in college. Nonetheless, he was still being recruited heavily by many big-time Division-I schools that wanted him to play both football and basketball. There were even some NBA scouts who came to his high school games. Many insisted that had he gone directly into the draft out of high school he would have certainly developed into a basketball star in the pros.

Moss announced that he had accepted a scholarship to play football at the University of Notre Dame. Located in South Bend, Indiana, Notre Dame is known worldwide for its outstanding academic and athletic programs. With his choice, Randy Moss had assured himself an amazing opportunity to excel with the nation's elite football players. Head coach Lou Holtz had recruited Moss in high school to come and play for the Fighting Irish. He had even come to watch Moss compete on several occasions. In the end, Coach Holtz got his man. Now all Randy Moss had to do was finish his last semester at DuPont, keep his grades up, and stay out of trouble.

Staying out of trouble was where Moss's plan ran into a snag that would forever change his future.

A two-time winner of the "Mr. Basketball" West Virginia Player of the Year Award, Randy Moss had many offers to play Division I basketball in college.

One day that spring, Moss was walking down the hallway at school. He saw that one of the white students had picked a fight with one of his black friends. Moss stayed close to back up his friend, in case the fight got out of hand. Then, as the two began to fight, Moss found himself getting pulled in. He lost his temper and began to help his friend fight. Maybe the heat of the battle had excited him, or maybe he wanted payback for all of the racial taunting he had taken from that particular group of kids for so long. Whatever the reason, Randy Moss was now involved in the fight.

When the fight was over, the police were called onto the scene. A group of kids blamed Moss. Moss, who had just turned eighteen years old, was criminally charged as an adult. Because Moss had accepted a scholarship to go to Notre Dame, and not the University of West Virginia, many of the local people were upset with him. They felt that he had rejected them. In their eyes Randy Moss was no longer the hometown hero they had once supported and rooted for.

To make matters even more tangled, Moss and his girlfriend, Libby, who is white, had recently had a baby girl named Sydney. Despite the fact that they were in love, many people in the community did not approve of interracial couples or of couples having children outside of marriage.

Moss pleaded guilty to assault charges for his part in the incident. He was sentenced to thirty days in jail, received probation, and had to perform community service work. He had made a mistake by getting involved in the fight, and he paid the price for his actions.

In an instant Randy Moss's world came crashing down like a house of cards. He was expelled from high school, and Notre Dame informed him that they had taken back his scholarship. The school claimed that the reason for taking back the scholarship was because Moss had failed to score high enough on his academic entrance exams. But many people suspected it was because of the incident. Everything Randy Moss had worked so hard for was now gone.

Randy Moss had hit rock bottom. But, then he got some good news. Head football coach Bobby Bowden of Florida State University (FSU) called to tell him that there was a scholarship waiting for him at FSU. Moss knew all about the Seminoles and their rich college football tradition. The school had been one of his top finalists before deciding on Notre Dame. The only catch would be that he would be redshirted, meaning he would not be able to play football during his freshman year. He hoped that if he stayed out of trouble and worked hard during his first year away from the football field, everyone would forget about the "incident" at DuPont. He wanted to be able to start over with a clean slate. He was elated, and could not wait to get out of West Virginia. He was going to college, and his dream of one day playing in the National Football League was one step closer to reality.

Chapter 3

College Years

Randy Moss got off to a good start at FSU. He was determined to make the most of his second chance. With no football during his freshman year, he worked hard in his classes. As soon as football practice started in his sophomore year, Moss quickly made an impression on his teammates and coaches. He ran an unbelievable 4.25-second 40-yard dash. This was an amazing time considering just how big of a player he was. (Up until that point, the fastest 40-yard-dash time ever recorded at Florida State was a 4.23, by then-cornerback and future Dallas Cowboy star Deion Sanders, who at the time weighed twenty-five pounds less and was four inches shorter than Moss.)

Randy Moss proved he was ready to step up and

play. He amazed nearly everyone in his scrimmages, scoring almost at will against the Seminole's first-team defense. Seemingly none of the FSU defenders could cover him. He put on show after show for the curious spectators who were now flocking to practice to see the new sensation. His popularity was soaring on campus, and people could not wait to see him on the field, when it would count.

The year ended with Moss going back home to West Virginia for the summer. There, he would train for his new role as the starting wide receiver for the top-ranked Florida State Seminoles. It appeared that Moss had redeemed himself, and was ready to take the world by storm. That's where the nineteen-year-old local celebrity messed up . . . again.

Randy Moss made a serious mistake that summer. The rules of his probation stated that Moss was to finish serving the suspended jail sentence from his prior assault conviction. He would attend the local West Virginia State College by day, to earn some more credits, and then report to jail at night. It was not the most comfortable arrangement, but it would last for just a few weeks—until he had fulfilled his punishment. Then he would be free and clear. Just a few days before he was to begin his sentence, Moss went out partying with some friends.

Shortly thereafter, he was required to take a mandatory drug test. He failed when traces of marijuana were discovered in his system. When his Florida State coaches found out about the test results, and that he had broken team rules by using illegal drugs, they decided to cancel his scholarship for the football team. Moss's probation was then revoked. The judge also tacked on an additional ninety days of jail time. His summer had gone from bad to worse, due to another poor decision.

Randy Moss paid, yet again, for a mistake. But his lifelong dream of playing college and pro football now seemed like it would never happen. Thanks to his poor judgement, he was now a castaway with no place to go. While he sat in jail that summer, he thought about getting back on the football field.

Two criminal incidents in as many years made him untouchable in the eyes of nearly every college and university football coach in the nation. There was one coach, however, who he thought he could call for another shot: former Florida State assistant coach Bob Pruett, who had just taken over as the head coach of Marshall University. Marshall, a Division I-AA school was located just west of Charleston on Interstate 64. (D-I-AA features smaller schools and is one step below D-I.) It was not as big and flashy as Notre Dame or Florida State, but Pruett was willing to give Moss one more chance to play the game.

"After a year of being red-shirted at FSU, Randy just needed to play football," said Pruett. "I knew Randy was a good kid, so I was eager to get him back onto the field—where he belonged. I knew that he was a tremendous talent and I'm just glad that I was able to give him another opportunity."[1]

Determined to turn his life around, Moss served his jail time and then enrolled at Marshall. He would be playing football for the Thundering Herd. Marshall did not have a prestigious football program like FSU or Notre Dame. But Moss planned to excel simply by playing at an entirely different level.

He came out more focused than ever that season, running over all of the defenders that stood in his way. Often double- and triple-teamed, Moss played like a man among boys. In his first game against West Virginia State, he hauled in 3 touchdown passes, and then added two more on 6 catches for 88 yards in his second game against Georgia Southern. His streak of touchdowns continued for the next three games until he had two touchdowns in games against both Western Carolina and Appalachian State. In the eighth game of the season, Moss lit up

FACT

During the spring of Randy Moss's sophomore season at Marshall, he decided to run on the school's track team. Despite not having raced competitively for more than four years, he won the Southern Conference Indoor Track 55- and 200-meter titles. His time in the 200 (21.15 seconds) was one of the best in the nation that year, causing some to speculate the he might have a shot at competing for a spot on the U.S. Olympic track team.

The Citadel for four scores on just five grabs. He followed that up with another pair of two-touchdown games against both Eastern Tennessee and Furman—where he combined for 14 catches for 312 yards. At 10–0, Marshall was soon becoming the talk of the D-I-AA football world—and the person that was usually right in the middle of those conversations was Randy Moss. He closed out the regular season by setting a freshman single-season receiving record by pulling in 19 touchdowns.

"If you were going to model the prototypical receiver, you would build Randy Moss," said Pruett.

> He's big, he's tall, he's strong, he's unbeliev-
> ably fast, he's very elusive when he runs, he's
> got great hands, he's got a great vertical leap,
> he's got great body control when he's flying in
> the air, he can make circus catches, he runs like
> a sprinter, jumps like a high jumper and after
> he catches the ball he runs like a running back.
> He's just got it all.[2]

In the playoffs, Moss took over and seemingly willed the Thundering Herd to victory. In the first game, a 59–14 win over Delaware, he set a school record by catching 8 balls for 288 yards and 3 touchdowns. Next up was Furman, who Marshall beat 54–0, thanks, in part, to a pair of touchdowns from Randy Moss. Then, in the national semifinals,

Whether it was catching the ball, rushing the ball, or returning it on punts and kicks, once Randy Moss got into the open field, he was almost impossible to catch.

Moss's rushing touchdown helped the Herd beat Northern Iowa by the final score of 31–14. At last, Marshall had made it to the Division I-AA National Championship Game against the University of Montana. There, Moss took over, catching everything that came remotely close to him. When it was all said and done, Moss had scored 4 touchdowns on 9 passes for 220 yards. Randy Moss had led the Herd to the national title and in the process, became one of the most talked about players in all of college football.

For the season, Moss hauled in 78 catches for 1,709 yards and 28 touchdowns—tying a Division I-AA touchdown record set by one of his boyhood idols, San Francisco 49ers star Jerry Rice, then of Mississippi Valley State. In addition, Randy Moss also led all college players with an average of 34 yards per return on kickoffs. For his efforts, Moss was named as a 1996 consensus First Team All-American. In addition to All-Conference honors, he was also named as the Division I-AA Offensive Player of the Year.

Happy to be near Charleston and his family, Moss had settled into his new setting. The fans were rooting for him again and he was thriving both as a player and as a person. Then, at the beginning of his second year at Marshall, something wonderful happened.

Thanks in large part to their championship football season of the year before, the school was allowed to move up to Division I-A status. Now, as a member of the Mid-America Athletic Conference, Randy Moss would finally have his chance to compete against many of the bigger, stronger football teams from all over the United States. It also meant coverage on national television and playing in larger stadiums where he could showcase his skills to a much larger audience.

Marshall's 1997 season opened against rival West Virginia, where Randy Moss made his Division I debut by hauling in 7 catches for 85 yards and scoring 2 touchdowns. His new partner on the field was sophomore quarterback Chad Pennington (a first-round draft pick of the New York Jets in 2000). Pennington passed to Moss early and often. Pennington and Moss would prove to be college football's most lethal pair that season. After losing the opener, the Thundering Herd roared back to win their next five games. Randy Moss scored on 79- and 90-yard bombs in Week 2 against Army, and then followed it up with a spectacular 216-yard, 3-touchdown performance in a 42–17 win over Kent State. In Week 4, Moss scored two more touchdowns against Western Illinois. He followed this with his best game ever—a 42–16 win over Ball

Thanks to 4 touchdown catches, Randy Moss led the Thundering Herd to the 1996 Division I-AA National Championship over the University of Montana.

State in which he had 13 catches for 205 yards and 6 touchdowns.

"They were playing him one-on-one and it just wasn't fair," joked Coach Pruett. "I mean his leaping ability and speed make him virtually unstoppable by just one person."[3]

Moss continued his pace over the next seven games. He had 107 yards on 6 catches for 2 touchdowns against Akron in Week 6. He followed that up with 10 catches for 147 yards and a score in a 45–21 loss against Miami of Ohio the following weekend. That would be the only blemish on the Herd's record from that point on. Marshall followed Randy Moss's winning ways all the way into the conference championship. Over the next four games—against Eastern and Central Michigan, Bowling Green, and Ohio—Moss caught 29 passes for 474 yards and 5 touchdowns. With just two losses, Marshall faced off against Toledo in the Mid-American Conference Championship Game. Behind Moss's 7 catches for 170 yards and 3 touchdowns, Marshall beat the Rockets, 34–14, to win the title. With the victory, Marshall, in just its first season of playing Division I football, was invited to play in the Motor City Bowl against the University of Mississippi. It

A "regular" on the evening sports highlight shows, Randy Moss was the biggest celebrity ever to attend Marshall University.

would be Marshall's first bowl appearance in more than fifty years.

On December 26, 1997, in Pontiac, Michigan, on national television, Moss and the Herd prepared to play the Rebels of Mississippi. The game was fierce, with a lot of early scoring. Moss was being double-teamed throughout the game, but still managed to grab an 80-yard touchdown bomb from Pennington late in the game. In spite of Moss's 6 catches for 173 yards, and a solid comeback attempt late in the game, the Herd lost, 34–31.

For Randy Moss, it was a bittersweet ending. He knew he was going to be fulfilling his dream of going on to the next level to play in the NFL the following year. He was sad, however, to leave many of his friends behind at Marshall. Moss's statistics were truly staggering. For the season he had caught 90 passes for 1,647 yards and 25 touchdowns—all conference records. His 25 touchdowns also set a new Division I college football record. (Moss also returned 14 kickoffs for 263 yards and 24 punts for 266 yards.) For his amazing efforts, he received the Biletnikoff Award as the nation's best receiver. He was named as a unanimous first team All-American and received Mid-American Conference Player of the Year honors.

Most significant though, Moss was named as

When the Motor City Bowl was over, Randy Moss knew that he was going to finally get his chance at becoming a star wide receiver in the NFL.

one of four Heisman Trophy candidates. The Heisman Trophy honors the nation's best college football player. Moss, Tennessee quarterback Peyton Manning, San Diego State quarterback Ryan Leaf, and Michigan cornerback Charles Woodson, were flown to New York City for the award ceremony. In front of millions of television viewers, Charles Woodson, in one of the closest votes in Heisman history, was named the winner. Moss finished fourth in the voting, but it had been a great honor to have been nominated. "With no disrespect to the other candidates, Randy should've won the Heisman," said Coach Pruett. "He was by far and away the best player in the country that year."[4]

Shortly after the season, Randy Moss announced he would be entering the 1998 NFL Draft. The draft is the way that NFL teams choose new players each year. Moss had been studying business at Marshall, but he decided it would be in his best financial interests to leave school early and start earning money in the NFL so he could take care of his family. His statistics told the real story. In just two short college seasons he had 168 receptions, 4,528 all-purpose yards, and 53 touchdown catches. It was time to move on to the challenges of professional football.

In just two seasons at Marshall University, Randy Moss scored 53 touchdowns, setting a new NCAA career touchdowns record.

"Randy played a key part in our program's successful jump to the next level," added Coach Pruett, who was sad to see him go.

> We were very excited that he was a part of our family. He has been good for Marshall and Marshall has been good for him. So, certainly to have a player of that stature play for us here, with all of the publicity that he brought to us, was an amazing plus for both him and us. He was a great, great player and no one gave this kid anything along the way—he's earned everything he's got. I have a lot of respect for him both as an athlete and as a person.[5]

Chapter 4

Landing in Minnesota

As Randy Moss prepared for NFL Draft Day in 1998, many football experts predicted that he would be a top-five pick. This would virtually guarantee him a contract worth millions of dollars. After tryouts with several NFL teams, all Moss had to do was sit back and wait for the results on draft day. But another bizarre incident brought his maturity into question yet again.

One evening, Moss and his girlfriend, Libby, had a heated argument. What started as a difference of opinion spilled outside onto the front yard of Libby's house. There, in front of some of the neighbors, the two could be heard yelling at each other. One of the neighbors called the police to report the domestic dispute. When the police arrived, they saw Moss and his girlfriend in the heat of their argument. The officers arrested both of them and charged them with domestic battery. The arrest came despite the fact that neither of them wished to file a complaint against the other.

Even after the two had resolved their differences, the damage had been done. Randy Moss once again found himself surrounded by controversy. With the draft just around the corner, many NFL teams decided to steer clear of someone who was now being labeled a "third-time offender." Many of the scouts saw Randy Moss as a potential troublemaker. They knew that he was the best receiver to come out of college football in perhaps the last decade. But they also wanted to be sure that if they invested in him they would not get a player plagued by personal problems and poor judgement.

Moss was not able to attend the NFL's annual combine because he had to get his wisdom teeth pulled. The combine is a two-day mini-camp where the nation's top college players all come together to do training tests and work out for all of the league's scouts and coaches. It is regarded as the most important of all the tryouts. While nearly every other highly regarded player about to be drafted was there, Moss's absence only led to further speculation. Many NFL teams were simply not willing to risk spending millions of dollars on a first-round pick they thought might get into trouble.

Finally, after months of suspense, Moss flew to New York to participate in the nationally televised NFL Draft. All of the top players were there. Moss knew that the two quarterbacks, Manning and Leaf, were going to go first and second, but after that it was wide open. Sure enough, Manning and Leaf were picked by Indianapolis and San Diego, respectively. The Heisman trophy winner, Charles Woodson, was picked next by Oakland. As player after player was selected, Randy Moss found himself still waiting to be chosen.

Twenty teams passed on Moss in the first round. He finally got the news he had been waiting to hear when NFL Commissioner Paul Tagliabue said: "With the twenty-first pick in the 1998 NFL Draft, the Minnesota Vikings select Randy Moss, wide receiver from Marshall University." His speed, strength, size, and spectacular leaping ability had simply made him too irresistible for the Vikings to pass up. Randy Moss's older brother, Eric, had also recently signed with Minnesota. The two would be reunited, just like old times back in Rand.

Minnesota had done its homework on Moss. Vikings head coach Dennis Green knew Moss had made some bad decisions, but he was willing to give him a shot. Coach Green knew that the Vikings, with many veteran players, would be a great place for Moss to mature and develop into a complete player. Minnesota would provide Randy Moss with a chance to start over and make a new beginning—far away from the problems that had plagued him in West Virginia.

"It's the best thing that could have ever happened to me," said Moss of being drafted by the Vikings. "If I would have been [drafted] in the top 10, it would have been a struggle. Here, I'm not in a situation where all the attention is on me."[1]

Randy Moss was headed for Minneapolis, where he would attend his first press conference as a member of the Vikings. Reporters were eager to hear about Moss's troubled past, but he was quick to point out that those days were behind him. He was just concentrating on doing whatever he could to help his new team make it to the Super Bowl.

Minnesota already had two of the best wide receivers in the league in Cris Carter and Jake Reed. With Carter and Reed performing at their usual high level, there would less pressure on Moss to succeed.

GETTING TO KNOW RANDY MOSS

Randy Moss is more than just a great football player. Away from the football field, he enjoys many fun and exciting things. Here are some of his favorite things:

Favorite Sport to Play (other than football): Basketball

Biggest Sports Thrill: Catching a touchdown pass and hearing the crowd go wild.

Favorite Color: Black

Favorite Actor: Steven Seagal

Favorite Movie: Any movie starring Steven Seagal

Favorite TV Show: *Crocodile Hunter*

Favorite Food: Breakfast cereal

Favorite Dessert: Cheesecake

Favorite Book: The Bible

Favorite Animal: Tiger

Secret Talent: Playing the drums.

Best Birthday Present I Ever Received: "A hug and a kiss from my mom."

FACT

Randy Moss's No. 84 jersey is so popular that many stores simply cannot keep it in stock. Between Thanksgiving and Christmas 1998, Moss's rookie year in the NFL, the Starter Apparel Company shipped more than 100,000 Moss jerseys to stores nationwide—the most it had ever shipped for a single player at one time. At one point, it was the NFL's best-selling jersey, ahead of Green Bay's Brett Favre, Dallas's Troy Aikman, and Miami's Dan Marino.

He could watch and learn at a slower pace while being taught by two of the game's best and brightest receivers. In addition to Carter and Reed, the Vikings also had quarterback Brad Johnson, and his backup, former league-MVP Randall Cunningham. Moss was especially looking forward to working with the quarterbacks. They both loved to throw long passes.

Moss could not wait to get started. Before the start of training camp, he decided to ask new team-mate Cris Carter if he could practice with him in Florida. Carter—an All-Pro and likely choice for the Hall of Fame—was very impressed that the rookie had sought him out before training camp even started. Moss was eager to speak with Carter. He knew that Carter had also had personal problems early in his career and that he had overcome them. Moss knew that if he just listened and learned, Carter would help show him the way.

"I was really excited when we drafted him," said Carter of Moss. "I knew that he was an outstanding player in college and was anxious to work with him out on the football field."[2]

Moss was amazed at just how hard Carter worked out. He also saw how professionally he conducted himself off the field. Moss knew that he had a new friend in Carter and he was grateful.

He also knew that he was going to be closely watched by the members of the media that year. Learning how to deal with that pressure before he got to Minnesota would prove to be invaluable.

Said Carter of Moss's maturity and development:

> I think it takes a lot of days, consecutive days, making the right decision. I think if he continues on the path that he is on now, his past will be behind him before he realizes it. But he has to realize that his past is not a myth. It is not something that the media has created. It is something that he brought upon himself. He realizes that. All he can control is what is going on today and what is going to happen in the future. If he wants people to stop asking him about his past, then he needs to continue to make good decisions on a daily basis.[3]

As Moss prepared for the start of training camp, he looked at the team's schedule for the upcoming season. The Vikings would be playing many teams that had passed on him on draft day. He was ready to prove that those teams had made a mistake.

When Moss finally did arrive at training camp, he was relieved to see that he was finally just a small fish in a very large pond. The Vikings team was loaded with superstar players. Despite the fact that

During the preseason, Moss made sure to listen and pay attention to the team's veterans as much as possible in order to learn the playbook.

the team had made the playoffs in 1997, it was in somewhat of a state of turmoil. The team was for sale, and many of the coaches were nervous about losing their jobs.

Texas billionaire Red McCombs bought the team after spy novelist Tom Clancy's bid fell through at the last minute. The first thing McCombs did was to sign all of the coaches to long-term contracts. This provided them, and everyone else, with a sense of security. Randy Moss felt much more at ease.

"When I showed up in Mankato for training camp, I got bombarded with questions," Moss said.

> You know, am I ready to go? Am I happy to be here? And my first answer was, "I'm ready to just play." And, day in and day out I just want to play well. I think I told Cris [Carter] I'm going to come in here and try to do the best I can to rip the NFL up.[4]

As training camp was about to start, Moss signed his first NFL contract. While many of his fellow first-round rookies decided to "hold out" for more money, Moss signed his contract fairly quickly. That way he could join the team for training camp and not have to worry about falling behind in his work. The terms of the contract were

Finally getting his chance to play in the NFL, Moss was all smiles at training camp.

not fully disclosed, but it was believed to be a four-year deal worth approximately $4.5 million, including a $2 million signing bonus. Moss could take care of his daughter and make sure that his mother would never have to worry about money again.

Moss enjoyed not being in the spotlight for a change. He decided to put all of his energy into making the starting lineup. He wasted little time in making a favorable first impression. As the players started to play some scrimmages among themselves, people quickly took note of Moss's amazing speed and confidence. He was routinely beating the defensive backs. Some of the players thought Moss's good fortune might be a fluke, but they quickly changed their minds when the Vikings played a scrimmage game against the Saints. Randy Moss scored 6 touchdowns.

One of the biggest adjustments that the Vikings quarterbacks had to make was not to underthrow Moss. Because Moss was so fast, their timing had to be completely different with him than it was with the other receivers on the team. Moss was also six feet four inches tall, and could outjump any defensive back in the NFL. The quarterbacks quickly learned to throw the ball up high and let him go up and get it. This secret weapon would open

Making spectacular one-handed grabs is just another day at the office for Randy Moss.

new doors that most offenses could only dream about. With three excellent receivers, Moss and Reed could now set up on outside routes, while Carter could line up in the slot to run shorter pass patterns over the middle. The trio quickly earned the new nickname "three-deep."

Chapter 5

The NFL Rookie of the Year

Fans in Minnesota had high hopes for the Vikings at the start of the 1998 season. Minnesota had finished with 9 wins and 7 losses in 1997, and had made a respectable run in the playoffs. They had beaten the New York Giants before losing to the San Francisco 49ers. The Vikings were on the upswing, and desperately wanted to keep the momentum going. "We feel like this is going to be our year," said Coach Green at the start of the season. "We've got a clear-cut goal for ourselves and that's to become the Super Bowl champions. We feel it's realistic. We feel it's attainable."[1]

The Vikings breezed through a perfect 4–0 exhibition schedule with wins over New England,

Kansas City, Carolina, and San Diego. Moss looked sharp in the opening preseason game against New England. He had 2 catches for 54 yards and he scored his first NFL touchdown. "The type of speed he has, I mean he's a threat every time he's on the field," said Patriots Pro Bowl cornerback Ty Law of Moss after the game.[2]

As the regular season was about to start, Moss learned that his brother, Eric, who had been sidelined with an ankle injury suffered during training camp, would be spending the season on injured reserve. Eric Moss would not play at all during the season due to his injury. But Randy Moss and the rest of the Vikings kicked off their season opener at the Metrodome, the Vikings home stadium, against Tampa Bay.

Moss wasted little time letting everyone from Minnesota know that he had officially arrived. He caught his first NFL regular season pass on the third play of the game. It was an 11-yard bullet from Brad Johnson. His next catch, two drives later in the first quarter, was good for a 48-yard touchdown. Johnson underthrew a long pass that most viewers thought would surely be intercepted by the opposing cornerback. Moss somehow turned in midair, came back for the ball, and bumped the ball up like a volleyball over the outstretched defender, back into his own hands as he landed in the end zone for the score.

Throughout the game, Moss's size and speed visibly intimidated Tampa Bay's defensive backs. Most rookies get hit coming off the line of scrimmage. This slows them down before they can get open. Moss was getting a 10-yard cushion of space. Defenders were giving the rookie speedster the kind of respect usually reserved for All Pro's.

The Vikings continued to roll against the Buccaneers. Moss and Johnson hooked up again midway through the second quarter on a 31-yard touchdown. This was Moss's second score of the day. Moss finished with 4 receptions for 95 yards and 2 touchdowns. Cris Carter added two more touchdowns, as the Vikings went on to crush the Bucs, 31–7.

Game 2 at St. Louis would prove to be a much more exciting contest. Moss did not score against the Rams. He did, however, impress a lot of people by putting on a bone-crushing blocking display that helped create three Minnesota touchdowns. The Vikings would need every one of those touchdowns in this game, as they held off the surging Rams on the last play of the game for a 38–31 victory. When quarterback Brad Johnson broke his leg during the game, backup quarterback Randall Cunningham

FACT

Randy Moss's older brother, Eric, who was signed by the Vikings in 1998, spent his entire first season on the injured reserve list with an ankle injury suffered during training camp. In 1999, the team sent Eric to play with the Scottish Claymores of NFL Europe—a developmental, or "minor league," team that is run by the NFL. There the big tackle got to play on a regular basis, honing his skills in preparation for returning to play in the United States.

calmly came in and hit Carter for a 19-yard game-winning touchdown.

Cunningham and Moss also connected immediately, hooking up for 2 touchdowns in wins over both the Detroit Lions and the Chicago Bears. Against the Lions, Moss caught 5 passes for 37 yards, including a 5-yard touchdown pass in double-coverage in the back of the end zone. Minnesota's defense held Detroit's All-Pro running back Barry Sanders to just 69 yards and guided the team to a 29–6 victory. Against Chicago, Moss proved to be the hero when he somehow leaped and hovered above a trio of Bears defenders to come down with a miraculous 44-yard come-from-behind game-winning touchdown catch on a pass from Cunningham.

In Week 5, the Vikings traveled to Green Bay, where Moss put on a show that left Packers fans utterly speechless. Moss used the nationally televised *Monday Night Football* game as his coming-out party. He had 190 receiving yards and 2 touchdowns. Green Bay's sold-out Lambeau Field was quiet after Cunningham threw for a record 442 yards, including 52- and 44-yard bombs to Moss. The Vikings rolled to a 37–24 win. "He's a big guy and has great leaping ability," said Packers safety

Against the Bears, Moss used every weapon at his disposal to get into the end zone, including a firm "stiff-arm" block to keep his opponent from tackling him.

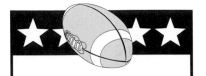

FACT

How did Randy Moss's rookie season compare to that of future Hall of Famer Jerry Rice's? Moss finished his 1998 rookie season with 69 receptions for 1,313 yards (a 19.0 yard average) and 17 touchdowns. Jerry Rice finished his 1985 rookie season with the 49ers with 49 receptions for 927 yards (an 18.9 yard average) and 4 touchdowns. Both won the NFL Offensive Rookie of the Year Award. Jerry Rice has gone on to earn three Super Bowl rings and a Super Bowl MVP award, something that Randy Moss is also hoping to accomplish.

Darren Sharper of Moss. "He doesn't play like a rookie, I'll tell you that."[3]

Game 6 saw the Washington Redskins and their veteran cornerback Darrell Green come to town. Green, long considered to be one of the fastest and best cover-men in the NFL, battled Moss up and down the field all day. The Vikings easily beat the Redskins, 41–7, but Green had shut down Moss, allowing him to grab only 5 catches for 64 yards.

The Vikings kept on cruising, as they traveled to Detroit for a rematch against the Lions. Minnesota got ahead early and was able to use its running game to tire the Lions' defense. Minnesota running back Robert Smith rushed for 134 yards in this 34–13 blowout. While both Carter and Reed scored, Moss was held to just 2 catches for 14 yards in the win. The Vikings rose to a league-best 7–0 record.

After losing to Tampa Bay, Minnesota won games against both New Orleans and Cincinnati. Moss was held to his lowest output of the season against the Saints, just one catch for 6 yards. He did manage to haul in 4 catches for 99 yards against the Bengals, though, including a spectacular 61-yard touchdown from Cunningham.

The Vikings were off to their best start since 1975.

Their offensive line was solid. Running back Robert Smith was having a great year. The defense was looking good, having allowed the second fewest points in the NFC (170). Cunningham, who was named as the NFC's Player of the Month for October, had emerged as the catalyst for this high-scoring offense. No one knew how to handle this potent air attack that was scoring at a record pace. Not even Brett Favre and the Green Bay Packers could get past the Vikings. As if to prove that his 2 touchdowns were not a fluke back in Week 5, Moss wowed the Metrodome crowd with 8 catches for 153 yards, including a 49-yard touchdown with 3:17 left on the clock.

Then, on Thanksgiving weekend, Moss gave Minnesota fans a whole bunch to be thankful for—a nationally televised 46–36 win over the Dallas Cowboys in Texas. Moss had performed like a champ before in the limelight. And this game will stand out forever as his breakout game. In an offensive explosion, Moss tortured the Cowboys for 3 fifty-plus-yard touchdown catches. He also drew a 50-yard interference penalty that set up another score. Dallas claimed that the loss came because their Pro Bowl cornerback Deion Sanders was out with a sore foot. Fans from around the country, however, had witnessed one of the greatest offensive performances in pro football history.

Moss, who twice received NFC Offensive Player of the Week honors and was the NFL Offensive Rookie of the Month for November, tried to keep it all in perspective. "I'm having a lot of fun," he said. "My individual goals I'll look back at when the season is over. Now, I'm trying to do whatever I can to go to the Super Bowl."[4]

The Vikings had won their divisional title. The home field advantage was secure. They went out and tried to have fun in their remaining few games. With the pressure off, Minnesota easily beat Chicago, 48–22. Moss scored 3 touchdowns on 8 catches for 106 yards. Proving he could be the "go-to guy," Moss stepped up as both Carter and Reed had to sit this one out with injuries. Moss's 3 touchdowns gave him a total of 14 for the season, breaking the NFL's rookie record. Opposing defenses were not able to cover him, and he knew it. "I wouldn't recommend a coach put his cornerback on me one-on-one with no help because that's either a catch, pass interference or a touchdown," said Moss.[5]

The Vikings cruised to easy victories over Baltimore, Jacksonville, and Tennessee, to finish the season with the team's best-ever regular season

Giving Minnesotans a lot to be thankful for on Thanksgiving Day, 1998, Randy Moss lit up the Dallas Cowboys for 3 touchdowns on 3 catches for an amazing 163 yards.

record at 15–1. In those final three games, Moss had a total of 14 catches for 193 yards and 3 touchdowns. For the season, Minnesota's offense had set a new NFL single-season record for total points, with 556.

After a well-deserved week of rest, with a first-round bye, the Vikings hosted the Arizona Cardinals in the NFC Divisional Semifinals in Minnesota. For Minnesota, expectations were at an all-time high. Anything short of the Super Bowl would be considered a failure. The Vikings were no strangers to the postseason. Coach Green had led them to the playoffs in six of the last seven seasons. Incredibly, however, they had just one win.

Feeling the pressure, Minnesota squashed the Cardinals, 41–21. The Vikings had earned a ticket to the final four of pro football, the NFC Championship. Moss led the charge for the Vikings over Arizona with 4 catches for 73 yards and a 2-yard touchdown grab. Next up for the Vikings were the Atlanta Falcons. They, like Minnesota, were used to playing on artificial turf in a deafening domed stadium.

The Falcons came into the Metrodome as the clear underdogs. But the Vikings had never won a Super Bowl in their thirty-eight-year history. In fact, they had lost four of them during the late 1960s and early 1970s. They were eager to earn another chance to win the big one.

The game got underway with Minnesota looking like it was going to win big. Cunningham was on fire, hitting Moss, Carter, and Reed all over the field. Running backs Robert Smith and LeRoy Hoard were carrying the load up the middle, and the defense was holding its own. The Vikings took a 20–7 lead into halftime, capped by Moss's 31-yard touchdown. But Atlanta battled back behind Pro-Bowl running back Jamal Anderson's punishing runs and a late touchdown.

Late in the fourth quarter, the Vikings had a chance to beat the Falcons once and for all. All they had to do was kick a 38-yard field goal to put the game out of reach. The good news was that Minnesota kicker Gary Anderson had set an amazing NFL record that year. He had not missed a single field goal during the entire season. The bad news was that his luck unfortunately ran out in the biggest game of his life. He missed the kick, and Atlanta, behind veteran quarterback Chris Chandler's third touchdown pass of the day, roared back to tie it at 27–27. With a minute to go in the game, Minnesota chose to take a knee on both third and fourth downs instead of going for a long

The dynamic duo of Randy Moss (left) and Cris Carter (right) are shown here. Will they both be future Hall of Famers?

bomb to win the game. The game went into overtime. Both teams failed to score on their opening drives. Then Atlanta came down the field and kicked a field goal to upset the Vikings, 30–27. Atlanta was going to Super Bowl XXXIII in Miami. More than 64,000 Vikings fans stood in complete disbelief. The players, like the fans, were devastated. "This [loss] will be with me until the day I die," said Moss.[6]

For Randy Moss, it was a sad ending to an otherwise brilliant rookie season. He had come in, pushed aside his bad-boy image, showed a lot of class and poise, and won the hearts of football fans everywhere. He made the most of his opportunity and was rewarded. For his efforts, Moss finished with 69 receptions for 1,313 yards (for an average of 19 yards per catch) and a league leading 17 touchdowns (10 of which came on plays over forty yards). He was named the Rookie of the Year. He also became the only rookie to be named as a starter for the NFC in the Pro Bowl in Hawaii. There he joined teammate Cris Carter for a week of fun and sun, and even managed to catch 7 passes for 108 yards.

"I accomplished most everything in my first year," added Moss. "The only thing I'm waiting on are some [Super Bowl] rings."[7]

Randy Moss, despite being six feet four inches tall and weighing more than 200 pounds, shows remarkable speed on the field.

Moss would have to keep up the hard work and wait another year to see if he and the Vikings could get to the Super Bowl. It would be hard to overcome the disappointment of coming so close only to lose. But Moss was determined to earn a Super Bowl ring.

Chapter 6

A Sophomore Season to Remember

Randy Moss went home and relaxed after the 1998 season, trying to put the Atlanta game behind him. He came back into training camp refocused and ready to lead his team back into the postseason in 1999.

"There was a lot of disappointment last year," said Moss. "A lot of disappointment in that Metrodome. I saw a lot of people moping, crying. I don't want to see it this year. I want to go to Atlanta [site of the 2000 Super Bowl]."[1]

Moss had reported to training camp that year acting more like a seasoned veteran than a cocky second-year player. He was more confident, more vocal, and more willing to do whatever it took to get his team to the next level. His teammates noticed the difference. "He's totally relaxed this year," said Carter of Moss. "He's adapted very well, and the guys have accepted him and he can really be himself. His understanding of the game is light years ahead of last year. He's a very, very good listener. He has God-given ability. His desire to be a great player is the thing that people don't see. But it's in him."[2]

For the first game of the regular season, the Vikings prepared to travel to Atlanta for a rematch against the same Falcons team that had beaten them back in January. Minnesota rallied to beat Atlanta, 17–14. Despite catching just 3 balls for 24 yards, Moss proved yet again to be a huge factor in the game's final outcome. Two pass interference calls on opposing players amounted to 76 yards, with each setting up Minnesota's only touchdowns on the day.

Game 2 was against Oakland, but reporters were focusing on the contest between Randy Moss and Charles Woodson. Moss and Woodson had both been Heisman Trophy candidates, with Woodson winning the honor. The two had become friends since then, making their showdown as "the league's top receiver versus the league's top cornerback" even more emotional.

"He won the Heisman; I should have won the

Heisman," said Moss to reporters. "People wanted to see me and him [face each other] coming out of college, and now you get your chance."[3]

The meeting between the two second-year players did not produce an afternoon of fireworks—just one amazing play that came midway through the second quarter. Randall Cunningham dropped back from the Raiders' 34-yard line and lofted a hanging spiral to Moss on the right sideline. Moss was running back toward the ball. He leaped over Woodson and somehow made a miraculous one-handed 29-yard grab to give the Vikings a first down at the 5-yard line.

"We're going to see it all year," said Woodson joking after the game. "I'll never be able to live it down. My boys are going to call me all week, saying it's the play of the day. He made a great catch."[4]

The Vikings fell apart after that big play, however. The Raiders scored on four consecutive drives to turn a 10–3 deficit into a 22–17 victory. For Moss, who caught 4 passes for 86 yards in the game, it was a bitter loss.

The Vikings traveled to Green Bay the following week to face the Packers. Green Bay had selected three tall cornerbacks with their first three picks of the 1998 draft.

Randy Moss made the catch of the year against Oakland Raiders cornerback Charles Woodson.

As a rookie, Moss had 13 receptions for 343 yards and 3 touchdowns against the Packers. He was held to just 2 catches for 13 yards on this day. One of those catches, however, a 10-yarder that put the Vikings on top 20–16 with just under two minutes on the clock, appeared to be the game winner. That was when Green Bay quarterback Brett Favre threw up a miraculous 23-yard game-winning touchdown on fourth-and-1 with 12 seconds remaining in the game.

"I was happy we had gone 80-some yards to score," said Moss of his touchdown. "But I knew we had to give it [the ball] back to the magician—and he worked his magic. . . . You can't start celebrating when they have Brett [Favre] over there," he added. "He's the MVP, man."[5]

With a 1–2 record, and Tampa Bay up next, Moss decided to take matters into his own hands. He caught a pair of 61- and 27-yard touchdown passes on the Vikings' first two drives of the game. Minnesota went on to beat the Bucs, 21–14. Moss's ability to score was the result of Vikings offensive coordinator Ray Sherman's attempt to move him around more between all three receiver positions. This would keep opposing defenses from keying in and double-teaming Moss. "During the off-season the coaches knew there was no more going down the sideline jumping over people, stuff like that," Moss said. "We just had to find another way to do it."[6]

The Vikings, despite a couple of wonderful performances from Moss, went into a slump after the game against Tampa Bay. They lost their next two games by just two points each to conference rivals Chicago and Detroit. Against the Bears, Moss managed to bring in 8 catches for 122 yards, but he was unable to score in the 24–22 loss for the Vikings. Against the Lions, Moss caught a career-high 10 passes for 125 yards and a touchdown in a 25–23 losing effort. "It was gut-check time for our team, and we let it slip away," said a dejected Moss after the game.[7]

Perhaps inspired by Moss's comments, the Vikings beat the San Francisco 49ers the following week, 40–16. Moss was held to just one catch for 24 yards. He found himself covered by two and sometimes three defenders throughout the game. As a result, newly appointed starting quarterback Jeff George (who took over for the slumping Randall Cunningham) did not hesitate to look in the direction of his other receivers, Cris Carter and Jake Reed.

The following week, the Vikings headed west to Denver, to face the two-time defending Super Bowl

FACT

Randy Moss and Cris Carter are truly a dynamic duo. In 1998, the pair broke the NFL record for touchdowns by a receiving tandem, with 29. They beat the old record of 27, which was set by San Francisco's Jerry Rice and John Taylor in 1989. In addition, the two combined for 2,654 receiving yards in 1999, the second highest total in league history—just 41 yards shy of the 1984 Miami Dolphins twosome of Mark Clayton and Mark Duper.

champion Denver Broncos. Denver, like the 49ers, opted to double- and triple-team Randy Moss throughout the game. Jeff George once again took his chances passing to Carter and Reed. Despite having only 3 catches for 39 yards, Moss still wound up right in the middle of the game's biggest play— catching a loose ball that had just been deflected off both Cris Carter and Denver cornerback Ray Crockett on a pivotal third-and-ten play late in the game. The play saved the drive and led to an emotional 23–20 Minnesota victory.

Next up for Minnesota was a *Monday Night Football* matchup against the Dallas Cowboys. Deion Sanders, the best coverage cornerback in the game, was healthy and going to be all over Moss. "I think it's going to be very big, and I think it's a chance for me to go against the best, and it's a chance for him to go against the best," said Moss of his matchup with Sanders before the big game.[8]

Dallas jumped out to a quick 17–0 lead. But when All-Pro running back Emmitt Smith was forced to leave the game with an injury, the Vikings made a comeback. Leading the charge was Randy Moss. His 6 catches for 91 yards and 2 touchdowns, including a spectacular 47-yard bomb from George with 5:10 remaining in the game, helped to rally the team to a 27–17 victory.

FACT

In 1999 Randy Moss announced that he might someday try out for an NBA team. He did not say exactly when he might do this. But he was immediately compared to a couple of other two-sport stars, Deion Sanders and Bo Jackson, who each played both pro football and baseball.

With momentum on their side the Vikings went on a roll, winning their next two games against Chicago and San Diego. Against the Bears, Moss was absolutely phenomenal, posting a career-high 12 catches for 204 yards, while teammate Cris Carter added 9 catches for 141 yards and 3 touchdowns, as the Vikings hung on to beat the Bears in a wild one, 27–24. For his efforts, Moss was once again named as the NFC Offensive Player of the Week.

After getting a much-needed rest over their bye week, the high-powered offense of the Vikings revved up and produced a season-high 485 yards in a 35–27 victory over the Chargers. Once again, Moss was unstoppable. This time he caught 7 passes for 127 yards, including a 37-yard touchdown. While the offense seemed to be back on track, the team's defense was causing Vikings fans to get nervous.

As the Vikings tried to continue their winning ways, they hit a couple of road blocks in both Tampa Bay and Kansas City. At Tampa Bay, Randy Moss was held to just 2 catches for 32 yards. The Vikings paid dearly for several turnovers that resulted in a 24–17 defeat. Then against the Chiefs, Moss showed the world that he was only human.

He dropped two passes and had two key

fourth-quarter fumbles while still managing to score 2 touchdowns. His first score of the day came late in the third quarter as Jeff George hit him with a 12-yard pass that tied the score at 21. His second touchdown came on a dramatic 64-yard punt return that tied the score at 28 with 1:38 remaining in the game. The Chiefs came back to win behind kicker Pete Stoyanovich's last-second field goal.

The Vikings beat the Green Bay Packers at the Metrodome, 24–20, in Week 15. Moss, as usual, was on fire, this time with 5 catches for 131 yards and 2 touchdowns, including a dramatic 57-yard bomb from Jeff George late in the second quarter. "I like big games," Moss said modestly. "That's how I'm made. I try to come out and always play [well] when the big games come."[9]

With their playoff hopes uncertain, the Vikings next traveled to the Meadowlands in New Jersey, where they took on the Giants. The highlight of the game for Moss was a play called "Z-pass-right," late in the third quarter. After Jeff George handed the ball off to Randy Moss on a reverse, Moss faked the run. Instead of running, he threw a perfect strike to a streaking Cris Carter for a 27-yard touchdown, and a 21–6 lead. The Vikings held on for a 34–17 win, guaranteeing them a spot in the postseason.

In the final regular season game of the year, the Vikings beat Detroit, 24–17. The game was important for Minnesota. With the win, the Vikings got home-field advantage in the first round of the playoffs. Although the game was tight, Randy Moss stole the show. A 67-yard touchdown pass highlighted his 155 receiving yards. Randy Moss had emerged as the team's go-to guy. "If the team wants to ride on my shoulders, all the way to the Super Bowl," he said, "then I'm going to have to take that challenge."[10]

Minnesota then hosted the Dallas Cowboys in the first round of the playoffs. The Cowboys would be out for revenge. Scoring in the game went back and forth. But, behind Robert Smith's team playoff record 140 yards rushing and Randy Moss's 127 yards receiving, the Vikings dug out of an early 10–3 hole. The Vikings scored the game's final 24 points, and advanced to the NFC's final four for the third straight season.

With the victory, the Vikings would face the St. Louis Rams in the second round. It would be a tough battle, but Moss was up for the challenge. "If it's a crowd taking a guy out, it means he's not focused," said Moss. "I like to play away more than I do at home."[11]

The Rams, much like the Vikings, were an explosive team with a high-powered offense. The Rams won, 49–37. The Viking had been ahead at halftime, 17–14, but they were completely outplayed in the second half. The Rams had a 35–0 second-half run that started with Tony Horne's 95-yard kickoff return for a touchdown.

Moss caught 9 passes for 188 yards and scored 2 touchdowns. But he could not do it all. As the game was winding down, the Randy Moss of old got angry. Late in the fourth quarter, a disgusted Moss complained to an official about what he felt was a blatantly blown pass-interference call on him. He then went over to the sidelines, grabbed a water bottle, and squirted the official. It was a childish reaction to a frustrating situation. The NFL commissioner's office responded sternly by fining Moss $40,000. Moss had used poor judgement in an uncomfortable situation.

Despite the ugly end to a frustrating 10–6 season, Moss had an otherwise brilliant second year. He finished with 80 catches for 1,413 yards (a new team record), and 12 touchdowns. He also earned himself a trip to the Fiftieth Annual Pro Bowl in Hawaii in 2000. He set two single game Pro Bowl records with 9 receptions for 212 yards. He also had a 25-yard touchdown catch from Carolina's Steve Beuerlein. Not surprisingly, he was named the game's MVP as the NFC defeated the AFC, 51–31.

"We had a lot of fun," said Moss of the Pro Bowl. "With Alstott [who ran for 3 touchdowns] rumbling through there, we did some good things. I'm not really into individual awards and things like that, but I guess I'll take them when they come."[12]

Chapter 7

The Future Is Bright

There is no telling just how good Randy Moss will be. Most people agree that he could be the first great receiver of the twenty-first century, and his future is bright. Randy Moss seems to have overcome his bad-boy image and proved his critics wrong. While he is confident, outspoken, even aloof, he is also hardworking, respectful, and honest. He has certainly made some mistakes along the way, but he has also paid for them. With hard work, he has turned his life around. Ever since he was a boy back in West Virginia, Randy Moss dreamed about one day playing in the NFL. Today he has not only reached his goals, but has surpassed them.

Randy Moss is a huge celebrity in the world of sports today. His face is on the cover of many national magazines, and he often appears as a guest on television shows. But he still makes time to give back. Charity and community service are both very important to Moss. With two children of his own, Sydney and Thaddeus, Moss enjoys working with and giving back to children. He works very closely with the Twin Cities community through several programs, including a personal favorite at St. Joseph's Children's Home called "Randy's Purple Pioneers." In addition to donating his time and services there, Moss visits regularly with sick and underprivileged children. He not only gives them gifts of signed footballs and jerseys, but also offers them hope and happiness.

With a sprinter's speed, incredible leaping ability, and soft hands, Randy Moss has truly taken the NFL by storm. In addition to being a talented offensive weapon, he has also become a terrific downfield blocker as well—often sacrificing his body for the good of his team. It was important for Randy Moss to establish himself as one of the game's best all-around players, not just a one-dimensional "go-deep-and-leap" receiver. Moss confidently lines up in the slot, runs crossing routes over the middle, goes in motion, carries the ball on reverses, and even throws passes for touchdowns. Nearly every opposing team double-teams him, rolls a safety to his side

Randy Moss is constantly surrounded by autograph seekers who want to meet him and shake his hand.

to prevent him from going deep, jams him at the line of scrimmage, and hacks at him up and down the field. Yet Moss seems to always find a way to get open. He is simply that good.

Many people have compared Randy Moss to one of his childhood heroes, San Francisco 49ers All-Pro wide receiver Jerry Rice. Both of them have the innate ability to adjust to balls in midair, both have great speed, and both can definitely blow a game wide open.

"If the situation is right for him, he's going to do a lot of wonderful things," said Rice of Moss.

> He's going to break records. He's shown every-body he's capable of making big plays, but now what I respect is I see him working under-neath a little more. That's the true mark of a receiver, to be able to catch the ball underneath and take a hit and to make plays.[1]

While comparisons to the game's greatest receiver of all time might be a bit premature, Moss under-stands his athletic celebrity in the world of sports-entertainment and embraces it.

As Moss sees it:

> I think that we're entertainers. And when [fans] see something they like, when they see a good entertainer—not meaning just athletics, but it could be music, country, rock, pop, what-ever you want to call it—if you give the people

FACT

Randy Moss has been in many television commercials, including one by Nike that takes us back to his West Virginia roots. In the commercial, Moss and his high school pal Jason Williams, now a star for the NBA's Memphis Grizzlies, are seen growing up as kids, playing basketball together at DuPont High and at college, and as stars in both the NFL and NBA. Playing in the background is the theme song from the old television show *The Dukes of Hazard*.

In 1998 Randy Moss smashed the NFL record for touchdown receptions by a rookie—which was 13—by hauling in 17 touchdowns.

something they like, they respond. Scoring three touchdowns with 200 yards receiving, when people see things like that, man, there's nothing but smiles. They like that. It's entertainment.[2]

Randy Moss has taken Minnesota by storm, and Minnesota fans have fallen in love with Moss. However, with the economics of professional football today, and the salary cap budget that teams must adhere to, it will be very costly to keep Moss in a purple uniform for years to come. In 2000, the Tampa Bay Buccaneers signed New York Jets Pro Bowl wide receiver Keyshawn Johnson to a record eight-year contract worth $56 million, with a $13 million signing bonus. Moss was in the third year of a four-year $4.5 million deal in 2000.

"As long as I'm connected with the Vikings, I intend for Randy Moss to be connected with them as well," said Vikings owner Red McCombs, who has no intention of letting Moss sign with another team as a free agent.[3]

Randy Moss will undoubtedly be remembered in football history as one of the great ones. An amazing offensive threat, he is that rare talent who can take a game over almost single-handedly. He has the whole package: quickness, toughness, passion, and intensity. Most importantly though, Moss is a role model to kids everywhere, proving firsthand that a lot of hard work, determination, and discipline—combined with pure, raw, talent—can be a recipe for success in life.

"I'm enjoying myself," said Moss. "Once you enjoy yourself, that's how life's supposed to be."[4]

Randy Moss had another All-Pro season in 2000, catching 77 passes for 1,437 yards (18.7 yards per catch) and 15 touchdowns, to lead the team back to its second NFC Championship Game in just three years. The Vikings opened the season by winning their first seven games, with the help of rookie quarterback Daunte Culpepper. Moss led the Vikings to a 30–27 victory over the Chicago Bears in the season opener. He had 4 catches for 89 yards, including a 66-yard bomb from Culpepper late in the game to seal the victory.

Moss's 15-yard touchdown pass with under two minutes to go gave the Vikings a 13–7 win over Miami in Game 2. After being shutdown against the Patriots in Week 3, Moss exploded for 3 touchdowns on 7 catches and 168 yards in a 31–24 win over conference rival Detroit.

From there Moss proceeded to score touchdowns in the Vikings' next four games. He had 21 catches for 322 yards in wins over Tampa Bay, 30–23; Chicago, 28–16; and Buffalo, 31–27; followed by the

FACT

Moss endorses several products for companies ranging from trading cards to his own line of cereal called "Moss's Magical Crunch." In addition, he has appeared in numerous television commercials for such companies as Snickers candy bars, Nike shoes, and *ESPN*, the magazine. Moss also stars in a Sega video game called "NFL-Y2K."

team's first loss, a 41–13 drubbing by the Buccaneers—a game which saw Randy Moss score on a remarkable one-handed "highlight reel" catch that somehow defied gravity.

In Week 10 the Vikings ventured to rival Green Bay, where they lost on one of the most bizarre plays in NFL history. With the score tied at 20–20 in overtime, Packers quarterback Brett Favre connected on a 43-yard touchdown pass to Antonio Freeman, which he bobbled on his shoulder, elbow and hands, all while falling down onto a rain-soaked Lambeau Field. But Vikings cornerback Cris Dishman forgot to touch him, in order to end the play. So, Freeman simply stood up and pranced into the end zone to score the dramatic game-winning score. For Moss, who had 160 yards on 6 catches, the loss was devastating.

Minnesota rebounded to win their next four games though, with Randy Moss leading the charge. He had 22 catches for 380 yards and 4 touchdowns in wins over Arizona, 31–14; Carolina, 31–17; Dallas, 27–15; and Detroit, 24–17. With an impressive 12–2 record, the Vikings were now virtually guaranteed a spot in the postseason.

Standing in Minnesota's way in Week 15, though, were the St. Louis Rams—the team that had knocked the Vikings out of the playoffs the year before. Moss's 4 catches for 63 yards and one touchdown simply were not enough. The Rams rolled over the Vikings, 40–29. Moss scored again the next week against Green Bay, but the Vikings lost the game in the final seconds, 33–28.

The Vikings then lost to the Indianapolis Colts, 31–10, in their final regular season game of the year. Randy Moss managed to provide one highlight though—catching a thrilling 42-yard touchdown pass from Culpepper late in the first quarter. With that, the Vikings, who earned a first-round post-season bye week, now prepared to do battle in the playoffs against the New Orleans Saints at the Metrodome.

Minnesota thoroughly outplayed the Saints, 34–16, to advance to their second NFC Championship Game in three years. Randy Moss caught a pair of 53- and 68-yard touchdowns from an injured Daunte Culpepper in the victory.

Poised to get back to the Super Bowl, the Vikings then headed to the Meadowlands to face the New York Giants in pro football's version of the Final Four. The heavily favored Minnesota Vikings got pummeled by the embarrassing score of 41–0. Moss caught just one pass for 42 yards.

After the game, Moss spoke candidly, with many of his comments outraging the fans of Minnesota.

"Do I think the Vikings can win a Super Bowl? I

don't know. . . . If I remain a Minnesota Viking, I'm going to do whatever is in my power to win the Super Bowl. If I'm not here, then I'm going to have to try to take the Super Bowl away from them."[5]

By the time training camp opened in Minnesota late in July 2001, Moss had signed the third richest contract in NFL history. The deal gives him about $75 million over eight years, including a record $18 million signing bonus. With Randy Moss locked up for the prime of his career in Minnesota, the Vikings' chances of finally winning a Super Bowl appear to look better than ever.

Chapter Notes

Chapter 1. Busting Loose in Dallas

1. David Scott, "Moss Hysteria," *Sport*, August 1999, p. 52.

2. Deanne H. Freeman, "Slippery Moss Eludes Cowboys," *State Journal Register* (Springfield, Ill.), November 26, 1998, <http://www.sj-r.com/sports/98/11/27/sa.htm> (February 2, 2001).

3. Ibid.

Chapter 2. Growing Up in West Virginia

1. John Rosengren, "Catcher on the Fly," *Spike*, Winter 1999, p. 14.

2. Author interview of Dick Whitman, March 15, 2000.

3. Ibid.

4. Author interview of Jim Fout, March 15, 2000.

5. Ibid.

Chapter 3. College Years

1. Author interview of Bobby Pruett, March 15, 2000.

2. Ibid.

3. Roland Lazenby, *Super Season: The Vikings' Unforgettable Year* (Banockburn, Ill:. HS Media Inc., 1998), p. 43.

4. Author interview of Bobby Pruett, March 15, 2000.

5. Ibid.

Chapter 4. Landing in Minnesota

1. Roland Lazenby, *Super Season: The Vikings' Unforgettable Year* (Banockburn, Ill:. HS Media Inc., 1998), p. 46.

2. Author interview of Cris Carter, March 25, 2000.

3. Lazenby, p. 46.

4. Ibid., p. 47.

Chapter 5. The NFL Rookie of the Year

1. Roland Lazenby, *Super Season: The Vikings' Unforgettable Year* (Banockburn, Ill.: HS Media Inc., 1998), p. 9.

2. Ibid., p. 10.

3. Ibid.

4. Ibid., p. 46.

5. John Rosengren, "Catcher on the Fly," *Spike*, Winter 1999, p. 16.

6. Jim Souhan, "Veteran Vikings May Not Have More Chances to Be Champs," *Star Tribune* (Minneapolis, Minn.), September 12, 1999, p. C1.

7. Kent Youngblood, "Lethal Weapon 2," *Star Tribune* (Minneapolis, Minn.), September 5, 1999, p. S1.

Chapter 6. A Sophomore Season to Remember

1. Kent Youngblood, "Bitter Loss Keeps Vikings Motivated," *Star Tribune* (Minneapolis, Minn.), August 2, 1999, p. C3.

2. Jim Souhan, "Healthy Moss Has Teammates Eager to Watch Him," *Star Tribune* (Minneapolis, Minn.), August 23, 1999, p. C1.

3. Jim Souhan, "Moss Takes Aim at Woodson," *Star Tribune* (Minneapolis, Minn.), September 16, 1999, p. C1.

4. Jim Souhan and Kent Youngblood, "Blocked Kick Hurt," *Star Tribune* (Minneapolis, Minn.), September 20, 1999, p. C1.

5. Jim Souhan, "Favre Upends Vikings 23–20," *Star Tribune* (Minneapolis, Minn.), September 27, 1999, p. C1.

6. Don Banks, "Vikes Show Bit of '98 Stardom in First Quarter," *Pioneer Press* (Minneapolis, Minn.), October 3, 1999, p. 1F.

7. Jim Souhan, "Moss More Concerned with Winning," *Star Tribune* (Minneapolis, Minn.), October 18, 1999, p. C3.

8. Jim Souhan, "Moss vs. Sanders: A Treat to Behold," *Star Tribune* (Minneapolis, Minn.), January 3, 2000, p. C3.

9. Don Banks, "George, Moss Lead Way Back from Special-Team Mistakes," *Pioneer Press* (Minneapolis, Minn.), December 21, 1999, p. 1F.

10. Jim Souhan, "Vikings Hurdle Lions, 24–17," *Star Tribune* (Minneapolis, Minn.), January 2, 2000, p. C3.

11. Jim Souhan, "A Look at a Long Rivalry," *Star Tribune*, September 25, 1999, p. C5.

12. Official NFL Web Site, "Randy Moss's Career Highlights—1999," © 2000, <http://www.sports.nfl.com/2000/playerhighlights?id=1679>, (February 2, 2001).

Chapter 7. The Future Is Bright

1. Jim Souhan, "Rice, Carter to Share Field for Perhaps the Last Time," *Star Tribune* (Minneapolis, Minn.), October 22, 1999, p. C3.

2. Robbi Pickeral, "Moss, Garnett: Two for the Money," *Star Tribune* (Minneapolis, Minn.), October 10, 1999, p. C1.

3. Kevin Seifert, "Suddenly, Moss' Status Is Worth a Look," *Star Tribune* (Minneapolis, Minn.), April 13, 2000, p. C4.

4. John Rosengren, "Catcher on the Fly," *Spike*, Winter 1999, p. 16.

5. Kevin Seifert, "Moss Not Backing Down From Comments," *Star Tribune*, (Minneapolis, Minn.) March 30, 2001, p. C3.

Career Statistics

Year	Team	Games	Receptions	Receiving Yards	Receiving Avg.	TDs
1998	Vikings	16	69	1,313	19.0	17
1999	Vikings	16	80	1,413	17.7	11
2000	Vikings	16	77	1,437	18.7	15
Totals		48	226	4,163	18.4	43

Where to Write Randy Moss

Mr. Randy Moss
c/o Minnesota Vikings
9520 Viking Drive
Eden Prairie, MN 55344

Internet Addresses

Official Site of Randy Moss
<http://www.randymoss.com>

Official Site of the Minnesota Vikings
<http://www.vikings.com/>

Official Site of the NFL
<http://www.nfl.com/>

Index

A

Aikman, Troy, 9
Alstott, Mike, 86
Anderson, Gary, 9, 69
Anderson, Jamal, 69

B

Belle, West Virginia, 15
Beuerlein, Steve, 85
Biletnikof Award, 40
Bowden, Bobby, 27

C

Carter, Cris, 9, 48, 50–51, 53,
        57, 61, 66, 69–72, 81,
        83
Chandler, Chris, 69
Clancy, Tom, 53
Clayton, Mark, 80
Culpepper, Daunte, 93
Cunningham, Randall, 8, 9,
        10, 50, 61–62, 64–65,
        69, 77, 80

D

Dishman, Cris, 93
Division 1-A, 36, 38
Division 1-AA, 31, 33, 35
Duper, Mark, 80
DuPont chemical plant, 13
DuPont High School, 15, 16,
        28

F

Favre, Brett, 65, 79
Florida State University
        (FSU), 27, 29, 32

Fout, Jim, 19
Freeman, Antonio, 94

G

George, Jeff, 80–81, 83
Green, Darrell, 64
Green, Dennis, 9, 48, 59, 68

H

Hall of Fame, 50
Heisman Trophy, 42, 76
Hoard, LeRoy, 10, 69
Holtz, Lou, 24

I

Irvin, Michael, 9

J

Jackson, Bo, 81
Johnson, Brad, 50, 60–61
Johnson, Keyshawn, 92
Jordan, Michael, 8

L

Lambeau Field, 62
Law, Ty, 60
Leaf, Ryan, 42, 47

M

Manning, Peyton, 42, 47
Marshall University, 31, 32,
        35, 40
McCombs, Red, 53, 92
Memphis Grizzlies, 19
Mid-American Conference
        Championship
        Game, 38

Mid-American Conference Player of the Year, 40
Mississippi Valley State College, 35
Monday Night Football, 62, 81
Moss, Eric (brother), 14, 17, 21, 47, 60–61
Moss, Maxine (mother), 13
Moss, Sydney (daughter), 26, 88
Moss, Thaddeus (son), 88
Motor City Bowl, 38
"Mr. Basketball," 22, 23

N

New York Jets, 36
NFC Divisional Semifinals, 68
NFC Offensive Player of the Week, 66, 82
NFC Player of the Month, 65
NFL Draft, 42, 45, 47

O

Ohio State University, 21

P

Payton, Walter, 14
Pennington, Chad, 36, 40
Pro Bowl, 69, 71, 85, 86
Pruett, Bob, 31–33, 38, 42, 44

R

Rand, West Virginia, 13
Randy's Purple Pioneers, 88
Reed, Jake, 48, 50, 57, 66, 69, 81

Rice, Jerry, 35, 64, 80, 90
Rookie of the Year, 71

S

Sanders, Barry, 62
Sanders, Deion, 8, 29, 65, 81
Sharper, Darren, 64
Sherman, Ray, 79
Smith, Emmitt, 10, 81
Smith, Robert, 9, 10, 64–65, 69, 84
South Bend, Indiana, 24
Stoyanovich, Pete, 83
Super Bowl XXXIII, 71
"Super Freak" sneaker, 8

T

Tagliabue, Paul, 47
Taylor, John, 80

U

University of Florida
University of Notre Dame, 24, 27, 32
University of West Virginia, 26

W

West, Jerry, 16
West Virginia State College, 30, 32
Wheaton, Kenny, 10
Whitman, Dick, 17
Williams, Jason, 19, 20, 22, 23, 90
Woodson, Charles, 42, 47, 76–78